ALBAN BERG, IGOR STRAVINSKY
and
ANTON WEBERN

Works for String Quartet

DOVER PUBLICATIONS, INC.
Mineola, New York

Bibliographical Note

This Dover edition, first published in 2005, is a new compilation of works originally published separately in authoritative early editions: Alban Berg, *Streichquartett* published by Universal Editions, Wien-London (1925); Igor Stravinsky, *Trois pièces pour quatuor à cordes* published by Editions Russe de Musique (1922); Anton Webern, *Fünf Sätze für Streichquartett* published by Universal Editions (1922).

International Standard Book Number

ISBN-13: 978-0-486-44292-1
ISBN-10: 0-486-44292-6

Manufactured in the United States by LSC Communications
44292604   2018
www.doverpublications.com

Contents

Alban Berg
(1885-1935)

Streichquartett
String Quartet
Op. 3

Igor Stravinsky
(1882-1971)

Trois pièces pour quatuor à cordes
Three Pieces for String Quartet

Anton Webern
(1883-1945)

Fünf Sätze für Streichquartett
Five Pieces for String Quartet
Op. 5

Instrumentation

1. Geige – **Violin I** – 1er Violon

2. Geige – **Violin II** – 2me Violon

Bratsche – **Viola** – Alto

Violoncello – **Cello** – Violoncelle

Alban Berg

Streichquartett
String Quartet

Op. 3

MEINER FRAU

Streichquartett

I

Alban Berg Op. 3

4

6

8

*) Vcl: Zeit lassen: unabhängig vom „A tempo" der drei andern Instrumente.

*) Im Tempo der korrespondierenden Stellen.

14

wieder ein wenig belebter, aber doch langsam.

ein wenig zunehmen. 170

*) Im Tempo der korrespondierenden Stellen.

15

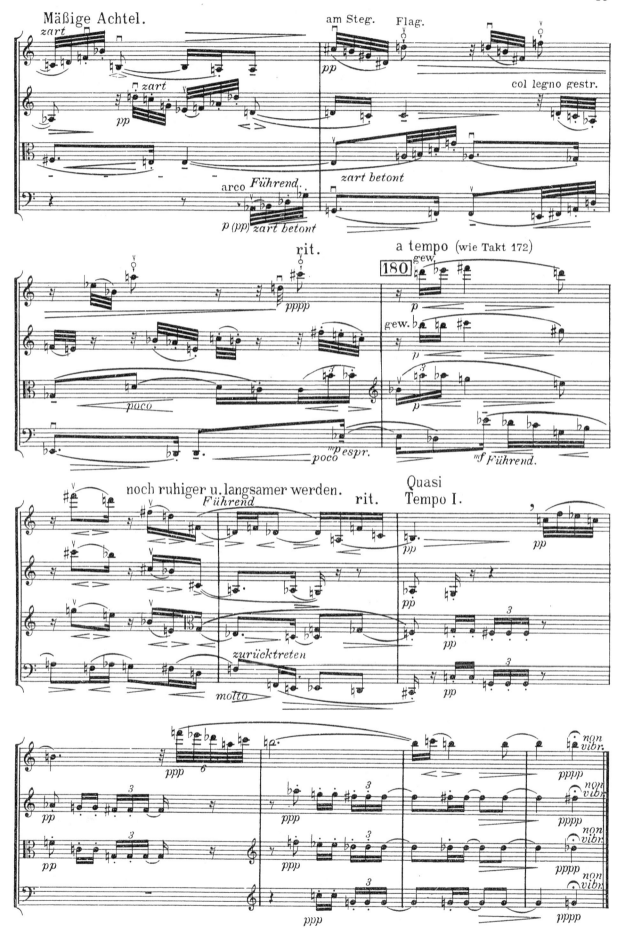

II.

21

24

26

*)Ausführung der Doppelgriff-Flag. *g–fis* (Br.) und *as–b* (2. Gg.)

Igor Stravinsky

Trois pièces pour quatuor à cordes
*Three Pieces for String Quartet*p

A Ernest Ansermet

Trois pièces pour quatuor à cordes

I

Igor Strawinsky
1914

34

35

II

★ Renversez vite l'instrument (tenez-le comme on tient un violoncelle) afin de pouvoir exécuter ce pizz., qui équivaut à l'arpège renversé.

III

40

sons réels

Salvan
1914

Anton Webern

Fünf Sätze für Streichquartett
Five Pieces for String Quartet

Op. 5

Fünf Sätze für Streichquartett

I

Heftig bewegt Tempo I (♩ = ca 100)

Anton Webern, Op. 5

II

III

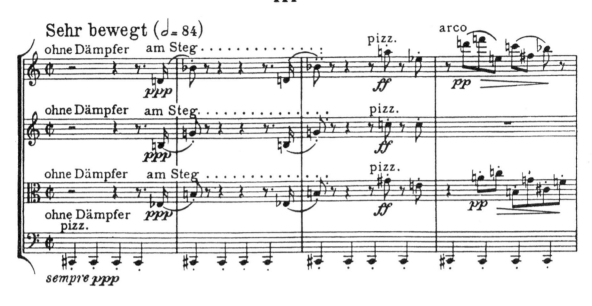

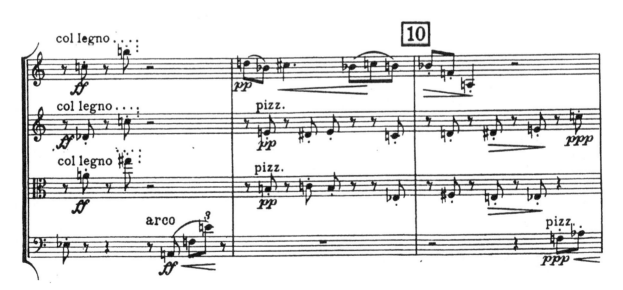

48

IV

V

Aufführungsdauer: insgesamt ca. 8 Min.

1909

Dover Chamber Music Scores

Bach, Johann Sebastian, COMPLETE SUITES FOR UNACCOMPANIED CELLO AND SONATAS FOR VIOLA DA GAMBA. Bach-Gesellschaft edition of the six cello suites (BWV 1007–1012) and three sonatas (BWV 1027–1029), commonly played today on the cello. 112pp. 9⅜ x 12¼.
0-486-25641-3

Bach, Johann Sebastian, WORKS FOR VIOLIN. Complete Sonatas and Partitas for Unaccompanied Violin; Six Sonatas for Violin and Clavier. Bach-Gesellschaft edition. 158pp. 9⅜ x 12¼. 0-486-23683-8

Bartók, Béla, STRING QUARTETS NOS. 1 AND 2. The stirring first quartet captures the composer's great stylistic rebirth, from the Romanticism of the opening movement to a finale inspired by Hungarian folk tunes. The second quartet combines disparate influences into a work of astonishing force and originality. 96pp. 83/8 x 11. (Not available in Europe or United Kingdom.) 0-486-43799-X

Beethoven, Ludwig van. COMPLETE SONATAS AND VARIATIONS FOR CELLO AND PIANO. All five sonatas and three sets of variations. Breitkopf & Härtel edition. 176pp. 9⅜ x 12¼. 0-486-26441-6

Beethoven, Ludwig van. COMPLETE STRING QUARTETS, Breitkopf & Härtel edition. Six quartets of Opus 18; three quartets of Opus 59; Opera 74, 95, 127, 130, 131, 132, 135 and Grosse Fuge. Study score. 434pp. 9⅜ x 12¼. 0-486-22361-2

Beethoven, Ludwig van. COMPLETE VIOLIN SONATAS. All ten sonatas including the "Kreutzer" and "Spring" sonatas in the definitive Breitkopf & Härtel edition. 256pp. 9 x 12. 0-486-26277-4

Beethoven, Ludwig van. SIX GREAT PIANO TRIOS IN FULL SCORE. Definitive Breitkopf & Härtel edition of Beethoven's Piano Trios Nos. 1–6 including the "Ghost" and the "Archduke." 224pp. 9⅜ x 12¼.
0-486-25398-8

Brahms, Johannes, COMPLETE CHAMBER MUSIC FOR STRINGS AND CLARINET QUINTET. Vienna Gesellschaft der Musikfreunde edition of all quartets, quintets, and sextets without piano. Study edition. 462pp. 8⅜ x 11¼. 0-486-21914-3

Brahms, Johannes, COMPLETE PIANO TRIOS. All five piano trios in the definitive Breitkopf & Härtel edition. 288pp. 9 x 12. 0-486-25769-X

Brahms, Johannes, COMPLETE SONATAS FOR SOLO INSTRUMENT AND PIANO. All seven sonatas—three for violin, two for cello and two for clarinet (or viola)—reprinted from the authoritative Breitkopf & Härtel edition. 208pp. 9 x 12. 0-486-26091-7

Brahms, Johannes, QUINTET AND QUARTETS FOR PIANO AND STRINGS. Full scores of Quintet in F Minor, Op. 34; Quartet in G Minor, Op. 25; Quartet in A Major, Op. 26; Quartet in C Minor, Op. 60. Breitkopf & Härtel edition. 298pp. 9 x 12. 0-486-24900-X

Debussy, Claude and Ravel, Maurice, STRING QUARTETS BY DEBUSSY AND RAVEL./Claude Debussy: Quartet in G Minor, Op. 10/Maurice Ravel: Quartet in F Major. Authoritative one-volume edition of two influential masterpieces noted for individuality, delicate and subtle beauties. 112pp. 8⅛ x 11. (Not available in France or Germany)
0-486-25231-0

Dvořák, Antonín, FIVE LATE STRING QUARTETS. Treasury of Czech master's finest chamber works: Nos. 10, 11, 12, 13, 14. Reliable Simrock editions. 282pp. 8⅛ x 11. 0-486-25135-7

Haydn, Joseph, ELEVEN LATE STRING QUARTETS. Complete reproductions of Op. 74, Nos. 1–3; Op. 76, Nos. 1–6; and Op. 77, Nos. 1 and 2. Definitive Eulenburg edition. Full-size study score. 320pp. 8⅜ x 11¼.
0-486-23753-2

Haydn, Joseph, STRING QUARTETS, OPP. 20 and 33, COMPLETE. Complete reproductions of the 12 masterful quartets (six each) of Opp. 20 and 33—in the reliable Eulenburg edition. 272pp. 8⅜ x 11¼. 0-486-24852-6

Haydn, Joseph, STRING QUARTETS, OPP. 42, 50 and 54. Complete reproductions of Op. 42 in D Minor; Op. 50, Nos. 1–6 ("Prussian Quartets") and Op. 54, Nos. 1–3. Reliable Eulenburg edition. 224pp. 8⅜ x 11¼.
0-486-24262-5

Haydn, Joseph, TWELVE STRING QUARTETS. 12 often-performed works: Op. 55, Nos. 1–3 (including Razor); Op. 64, Nos. 1–6; Op. 71, Nos. 1–3. Definitive Eulenburg edition. 288pp. 8⅜ x 11¼. 0-486-23933-0

Mendelssohn, Felix, COMPLETE CHAMBER MUSIC FOR STRINGS. All of Mendelssohn's chamber music: Octet, Two Quintets, Six Quartets, and Four Pieces for String Quartet. (Nothing with piano is included.) Complete works edition (1874–7). Study score. 283pp. 9⅜ x 12¼. 0-486-23679-X

Mozart, Wolfgang Amadeus, COMPLETE STRING QUARTETS. Breitkopf & Härtel edition. All 23 string quartets plus alternate slow movement to K.156. Study score. 277pp. 9⅜ x 12¼. 0-486-22372-8

Mozart, Wolfgang Amadeus, COMPLETE STRING QUINTETS, Wolfgang Amadeus Mozart. All the standard-instrumentation string quintets, plus String Quintet in C Minor, K.406; Quintet with Horn or Second Cello, K.407; and Clarinet Quintet, K.581. Breitkopf & Härtel edition. Study score. 181pp. 9⅜ x 12¼. 0-486-23603-X

Ravel, Maurice, PIANO TRIO, MALLARMÉ POEMS AND OTHER CHAMBER WORKS. The celebrated Piano Trio of 1914, the Mallarmé Poems (1913), Sonata for Violin and Cello (1922), and Introduction and Allegro (1905) for harp and ensemble appear in this first-time collection of some of the composer's finest and most musically ambitious achievements in a single large-format volume. 128pp. 8⅜ x 11. (Not available in France or Germany)
0-486-43807-4

Schoenberg, Arnold, CHAMBER SYMPHONY NO. 1 FOR 15 SOLO INSTRUMENTS, OP. 9. One of Schoenberg's most pleasing and accessible works, this 1906 piece concentrates all the elements of a symphony into a single movement. 160 pp. 8⅜ x 11. (Available in U.S. only) 0-486-41900-2

Schubert, Franz, COMPLETE CHAMBER MUSIC FOR PIANOFORTE AND STRINGS. Breitkopf & Härtel edition. Trout, Quartet in F Major, and trios for piano, violin, cello. Study score. 192pp. 9 x 12. 0-486-21527-X

Schubert, Franz, COMPLETE CHAMBER MUSIC FOR STRINGS. Reproduced from famous Breitkopf & Härtel edition: Quintet in C Major (1828), 15 quartets and two trios for violin(s), viola, and violincello. Study score. 348pp. 9 x 12. 0-486-21463-X

Schumann, Clara (ed.), CHAMBER MUSIC OF ROBERT SCHUMANN, Superb collection of three trios, four quartets, and piano quintet. Breitkopf & Härtel edition. 288pp. 9⅜ x 12¼. 0-486-24101-7

Stravinsky, Igor, PRIBAOUTKI, RENARD AND RAGTIME FOR ELEVEN INSTRUMENTS. Pribaoutki (Nonsense Rhymes) is a set of four witty, brief songs for solo voice and eight solo instruments; Renard, adapted from Russian folktales, features talking animals; and Ragtime for Eleven Instruments reflects the composer's interest in the contemporary jazz idiom. Texts in Russian, French, German. 224pp. 8⅜ x 11. (Available in U.S. only)
0-486-41395-0

Tchaikovsky, Peter Ilyitch, PIANO TRIO IN A MINOR, OP. 50. Charming homage to pianist Nicholas Rubinstein. Distinctively Russian in character, with overtones of regional folk music and dance. Authoritative edition. 120pp. 8⅛ x 11. 0-486-42136-8

Tchaikovsky, Peter Ilyitch and Borodin, Alexander, COMPLETE STRING QUARTETS. Tchaikovsky's Quartets Nos. 1–3 and Borodin's Quartets Nos. 1 and 2, reproduced from authoritative editions. 240pp. 8⅜ x 11¼. 0-486-28333-X

Available from your music dealer or write for free Music Catalog to
Dover Publications, Inc., Dept. MUBI, 31 East 2nd Street, Mineola, NY 11501
Visit us online at www.doverpublications.com